PEACE

FEARLESS RESILIENCE
IN A CHAOTIC WORLD

PAT HARRISON

Published by Harrison House Publishers
Shippensburg, PA 17257

ISBN 13 TP: 978-1-6675-0316-5
ISBN 13 eBook: 978-1-6675-0317-2

For Worldwide Distribution, Printed in the U.S.A.
1 2 3 4 5 6 7 8 / 27 26 25 24 23

CONTENTS

INTRODUCTION

Every believer should be enjoying a life of peace, because this is what Jesus offers us. The peace Jesus offers is nothing like what the world offers. It is a deep sense of knowing that passes all understanding, regardless of what is going on in front of us. The peace the world offers is temporary because it is based on what you have and if everything in life is going the way you want it to. Worldly peace disappears once things are not going your way. If your life is moved by circumstances, you will never know stability. The peace Jesus offers us operates in good times or bad. His peace operates in the dark of the night, in the midst of a storm!

Our peace is multiplied to us in our knowledge of God (see 1 Peter 1:2). We can expect that as we grow in knowing Him, our peace grows as well. Peace is an indicator of our growth. Like everything else God offers us, we receive peace by faith, standing on what we know God has promised. This is why knowing what God has said about the peace He offers us is important; it adds to the Holy Spirit's arsenal of what He can stir in us when we need peace. We need the Word on peace and the Spirit of peace in our lives! When we allow the Word and the Spirit to operate in our life, peace is the result. God intends that a life of peace be our portion.

To be in faith is to be at peace. Frustration and struggle are the result of trying to control things in the natural that you cannot do anything about. There is no room for strife and stress in the Spirit!

> *But among the Israelites it will be so peaceful that not even a dog will bark. Then you will know that the Lord makes a distinction between the Egyptians and the Israelites* (Exodus 11:7 NLT).

Faith is how we receive from God and peace is the position we maintain while we await the manifestation of our faith. The peace of God is not dependent on the absence of challenges in our lives. The peace of God is our anchor through the challenges that will enable us to sail through the other side. Peace is a shield around us in the midst of any challenge that the enemy tries to bring our way.

The enemy wants to steal our peace because the only way he can get to us is if we are not in peace. The Holy Spirit works in an atmosphere of peace. The enemy works in an atmosphere of turmoil. This is why Jesus offered us His peace: so we can have the Holy Spirit in operation in our life at all times. His peace is our strength. When we choose peace, we are choosing to go ahead with our life while God works on our behalf.

For to us a Child is born, to us a Son is given; and the government shall be upon His shoulder, and His name shall be called Wonderful Counselor, Mighty God, Everlasting Father [of Eternity], Prince of Peace (Isaiah 9:6 AMPC).

There is no stress and strain in faith. Peace is the rightful position of the believer because peace is a gift that Jesus Himself has left us.

In a world so desperately seeking peace, God offers us peace as a guard for our hearts and minds.

Chapter 1

NO PEACE

When I was a child, I wasn't afraid to play in the front yard or walk down the street without adult supervision. The library, school, department store, and movie theater were safe places to go. We weren't concerned about bullets flying through the air, bombs exploding, or terrorists hijacking airplanes.

The world is a vastly different place today. But in truth, the world hasn't been a safe place since Adam and Eve allowed sin to enter the Garden of Eden (see Genesis 3).

God created the world and gave Adam the authority and power to administrate it (see Genesis 1:26). Because the Lord was present every day in the Garden and sin wasn't present, it was a peaceful and beautiful place. But the peace disappeared when Adam and Eve sinned.

Since that time, the world has experienced civil wars, world wars, famine, plagues, floods, fires, holocausts, and ethnic cleansings. It just seems as if these things have gotten worse because we are closer to the end of time.

Regardless of how many laws and regulations governments put in place, or how many police officers patrol the streets, or how many organizations are formed to promote peace, the world will never have peace because of sin.

If we cannot find peace through man's efforts, where can we find peace?

In the midst of Jerusalem, a historically contentious city ruled by Rome, Jesus Christ spoke of peace. This was a peace that no government or culture could guarantee. His promise of peace stood in stark contrast to the *Pax Romana* or Roman peace begun by Caesar Augustus, who ruled the Roman Empire from 30 B.C. until he died, fourteen years after the birth of Jesus.

In those days, the Roman rule offered many benefits. It established a monetary system, codified law through its vast empire, and built highways and aqueducts. In the Book of Acts, Paul boasted to the Roman commander of his Roman citizenship: "*The commandant replied, I purchased this citizenship [as a capital investment] for a big price. Paul said, But I was born [Roman]!*" (Acts 22:28 AMPC). The *Pax Romana* enabled Paul and the other disciples to spread the gospel.

It was the set time for Jesus to come so that God could extend true peace to mankind.

Since many nations or groups came under Roman rule, much of the world enjoyed a pause from warfare. However, those who were conquered knew the price of Roman peace—excessive taxation, crucifixions, beatings, imprisonment, and slavery. It wasn't true peace.

Caesar Augustus commissioned Roman sculptors to build the *Ara Pacis,* the Altar of Peace, to celebrate his establishment of peace. That altar still stands in Rome today, and its existence mocks the inability of man to give the world peace. This Roman ruler knew unparalleled power, wealth, and worldly peace in his lifetime. But in his death, he had no peace—no presence of God.

To bring peace back to mankind, God gave His best—Jesus.

> *For to us a Child is born, to us a Son is given; and the government shall be upon*

His shoulder, and His name shall be called Wonderful Counselor, Mighty God, Everlasting Father [of Eternity], Prince of Peace (Isaiah 9:6 AMPC).

Jesus, the Prince of peace, is our peace.

Peace I leave with you; My [own] peace I now give and bequeath to you. Not as the world gives do I give to you. Do not let your hearts be troubled, neither let them be afraid (John 14:27 AMPC).

Chapter 2

WHAT IS PEACE?

The word *peace* carried a negative meaning in the Greek language, because it spoke of the absence of problems, tragedies, and so on. But in the Hebrew language, the word *peace* carried a positive connotation. It didn't represent the absence of a problem, but rather the presence of something to keep you in peace. It spoke of a blessing that resulted from a right relationship with God.

The word *peace* was commonly used in New Testament times as a greeting or farewell. We no longer use it in this manner today. We say "goodbye," which is actually a form of "God be with you," because the world can only *hope* that God is with them. John 14:27 (AMPC) says: "*Peace I leave with you; My [own] peace I now give and bequeath to you. Not as the world gives do I give to you. Do not let your hearts be troubled, neither let them be afraid. [Stop allowing yourselves to be agitated and disturbed; and do not permit yourselves to be fearful and intimidated and cowardly and unsettled.]*" Jesus promised a supernatural peace to His disciples.

The word for *peace* in John 14:27 is the Greek word *eirene*, which is a term used in greetings and farewells. But this was not the ordinary farewell of a master to his disciples. Jesus' peace was no less than the presence and power of God in one's life because of receiving salvation.

Jesus came to earth, died on the cross, and rose again to bring us peace.

The Message Bible translates John 14:27 this way, "*I'm leaving you well and whole. That's my parting gift to you. Peace. I don't leave you the way you're used to being left—feeling abandoned, bereft. So don't be upset. Don't be distraught.*"

> *In peace I will lie down and sleep, for you alone, O Lord, will keep me safe* (Psalm 4:8 NLT).

Peace is defined as "tranquility of heart and tranquility of mind." *Tranquility* or *peace* also means "a quietness and a rest." It is perfect well-being because we are in a right relationship with God through Jesus Christ.

You might be thinking, *How can I be peaceful when I'm in the middle of a mess? I've got problems.* You must remember that peace isn't the absence of messes and problems. Peace is the presence of Jesus in the midst of the mess. Your heart and your mind can be tranquil even in the midst of tragedy. I know because I've been there many times.

Sometimes when we are just thinking about and meditating on peace, we need to say *peace, peace, peace*. As we speak these words, peace will come, and we will become aware of the quietness and rest that comes *around* us, *in* us, and *through* us.

In the day we live in now, it's even more important to maintain our peace. All of the pressures in life are real and can't be ignored. But when things go wrong, we cannot allow the pressures of the world to steal our joy and our peace. The world's peace is temporary, fleeting, and unreliable. No worldly system can guarantee lasting peace.

Today, many people, including Christians, are not experiencing peace in their lives. Some people *think* they can find peace in a bottle or pill, or sitting cross-legged on a mountainside chanting a mantra. Others try to find peace by escaping to the wilderness. But peace is not a thing or a process; it is a *person—Jesus Christ.*

Are you at peace? Are you living in peace? Is there peace in your heart? Unsaved people can only hope they will have peace, but Jesus didn't say, "My peace I hope you have." He said He *gives* us peace and *leaves* it with us.

The lowly will possess the land and will live in peace and prosperity (Psalm 37:11 NLT).

In John 14:27, Jesus was making a bequest. A bequest is something left by a will. God's will is the New Testament—His covenant with us. The peace that Jesus gives is the natural result of the Holy Spirit's presence within us. Peace is Jesus' bequest to His disciples.

The expression that Jesus used in John 14:27 was not the common usage of the word *peace*. He used this term in His own way, for His own purpose. By His reputation, Jesus emphasized the importance of peace. He said that He gives peace and then continued to say that His peace was not like the peace the world gives.

When Jesus died and rose again, He came forth as the Prince of Peace. Since He is the Prince of Peace and lives on the inside of us, when He speaks peace is created in us.

If you have received Jesus Christ as your Lord and Savior, you have peace.If you have never received Jesus as your Lord and Savior, there is no better time than right now. Just pray this simple prayer:

> *Father, I admit that I have sinned. I need You, and I believe that Jesus is Your Son and Savior. I receive Your forgiveness. I accept Jesus as my Lord*

*and Savior. Thank You. In Jesus'
Name, amen.*

Now that Jesus is your Lord and Savior, you
have peace and you can walk in it every day.

*And God purposed that through
(by the service, the intervention
of) Him [the Son] all things
should be completely reconciled
back to Himself, whether on
earth or in heaven, as through
Him, [the Father] made peace
by means of the blood of His
cross* (Colossians 1:20 AMPC).

Chapter 3

UNPEACE

One of the reasons we experience unrest and "unpeace" is because we don't listen to God and focus on His Word. Instead we listen to worldly opinions and the voice of our feelings and then we think on wrong thoughts. We worry on the problem instead of meditating on the promise.

I am not saying that we ignore reality. Life is messy. We will have few, if any, days when we don't face a problem, a difficulty, a challenge, or a tragedy. It isn't that God wants us to ignore these things. He just wants us to focus on a higher reality—the truth of His report. He wants us to focus on Jesus and the promises of the Word.

When we give place to Jesus' presence, power, and promise, the feelings of unrest and "unpeace" will leave and the "feelings" of peace will flood us. Understand this: There is nothing wrong with feelings. We aren't bad or sinful because we have feelings. God has emotions, and He created us to have emotions. We just need to keep them in their proper place, and that proper place is in subjection to the Spirit and Word of God. Feelings are not supposed to control us; we are supposed to control them.

The battle to steal our peace begins in the mind. The feelings of unrest, "unpeace," and insecurity start to flood our souls when we begin to give place to the enemy's lies. He bombards us with wrong thoughts: *What if? How will I ever get through this? I don't know what I'm going to do.*

> *He lets me rest in green meadows; he leads me beside peaceful streams* (Psalm 23:2 NLT).

We become insecure and fearful when we don't allow Jesus to be what He said He would be to us—when we don't allow Him to work in our lives. As a result, we begin to walk down the path of unrest and "unpeace." Then everything seems to fall apart.

Do you believe that your Father God is all-knowing, all-powerful, and always present with you? Do you believe He created the entire universe and holds it all together by the power of His Word? Do you believe Jesus fed more than 5,000 people with a few pieces of fish and bread? Do you believe He healed the sick and raised the dead? Do you believe that Jesus rose from the dead and is now alive forevermore and seated at the Father's right hand praying for you?

I am sure that you confidently and boldly answered "yes" to all those questions. So let me ask you another question: Is whatever you are facing harder for God to do than anything He has already done? I trust that your answer is "no." Therefore, why are you distressed, anxious, and fearful?

Because you are thinking on the wrong things. You are trying to figure out how to solve your problems in your own strength and abilities. You are trying to figure out what man or government agency you can go to for help. Instead of trying to figure things out on your own, you need to let God be God in your life.

You need to come back to the Word of God and say, *Lord, I repent for allowing myself to get in this place.* When you come back to the Word of God and say, *I know His Word is truth and it's His truth that makes me peaceful and causes me to walk the way I should walk*, then peace will come. Peace doesn't come because of what you have done in the natural. Peace comes because you know that Jesus is on the inside of you and you have spoken His truth.

We cannot expect to find peace in the world's system because the devil is the ruler of this world. Thus, the world's values, philosophies, mindset, and priorities are contrary to God's will and ways. Since peace is only available in a relationship with Jesus Christ, unsaved people are not going to have peace. Therefore, unrest, fear, turmoil, strife, and insecurity will prevail in the world until Jesus' triumphant return as King of kings and Lord of lords. There's no greater peace than the peace of God through Jesus Christ.

For He is [Himself] our peace (our bond of unity and harmony). He has made us both [Jew and Gentile] one [body], and has broken down (destroyed, abolished) the hostile dividing wall between us, by abolishing in His [own crucified] flesh the enmity [caused by] the Law with its decrees and ordinances [which He annulled]; that He from the two might create in Himself one new man [one new quality of humanity out of the two], so making peace (Ephesians 2:14-15 AMPC).

And God purposed that through (by the service, the intervention of) Him [the Son] all things should be completely reconciled back to Himself, whether on earth or in heaven, as through Him, [the Father] made peace by means of the blood of His cross (Colossians 1:20 AMPC).

When Jesus is your Lord and Savior, you have peace with God. He's not mad at you. God's not looking for a reason to punish you. He loves you. That's what Colossians 1:20 means. Now every day you must choose to walk in Jesus' peace by faith.

So God has given both his promise and his oath. These two things are unchangeable because it is impossible for God to lie. Therefore, we who have fled to him for refuge can have great confidence as we hold to the hope that lies before us (Hebrews 6:18 NLT).

Chapter 4

CIRCUMSTANTIAL VERSUS SUSTAINING PEACE

Jesus offers more than hope. Unlike the peace the world offers, His peace depends solely upon Himself—the unchanging, eternal, all-powerful one. His peace is not dependent on outward circumstances. The world delivers circumstantial peace, which is based on needs being met or on good circumstances surrounding us in our lives. For instance, ministers experience circumstantial peace when their churches are doing well, their attendance is up, their Bible schools are well-funded, and their incomes are adequate. Another example of circumstantial peace is when we have lots of money in the bank or when we get good medical reports from the doctors.

Circumstantial peace is fleeting or temporary because it is shattered by the intrusion of the unknown or unwanted. For instance, someone might ask for prayer for peace and receive it, but that peaceful feeling will only last a short period of time if that person tries to find it on a circumstantial level. In other words, one can "feel" the peace of God and receive it as long as one's circumstances look okay.

The peace of Jesus is not based on circumstances or feelings; it's based on His person, character, and nature—the eternal, unchanging, trustworthy, faithful, and all-powerful Son of God. In the midst of fiery trials, He tells us not to let our hearts be troubled. His peace is a Christ-centered serenity that is established upon the absolutes of His Word.

In the world we will always have trouble and sometimes distressing, chaotic, and uncontrollable circumstances. But we cannot let our peace depend on our circumstances. It must depend solely on the presence of God. Jesus said it was good that He would go away because another comforter would come in His place. The Holy Spirit is our comforter, advocate, and standby. He is God's agent for maintaining peace in our lives. We can walk in peace and maintain it in our lives when we choose to dwell on the promises of God rather than our circumstances.

When fear, anxiety, doubt, or unbelief attacks us, we must make the decision either to practice the absence or presence of God in our lives. I know it is possible to experience His peace every day regardless of circumstances or feelings because I practice God's presence and peace every day.

As parents of three children, my husband and I learned to rely on the Lord as we reared them, particularly when they became teenagers, started driving, and could go out on their own. One night one of our children missed curfew. In those days since we didn't have cell phones, we couldn't call or text to find out what was going on. By the time 30 to 40 minutes had passed, Buddy and I were getting anxious and upset.

I had all these thoughts about what could have happened to my child running through my mind and trying to produce fear, worry, and anger. The moment I realized that my emotions were trying to take over, I started praying in the Spirit. I began refusing those wrong thoughts and said to the Lord, *You know where my child is. You know what's going on. I trust You, and I ask You to help me.* I started praising and thanking Him for His protection and peace. I began quoting the promises from His Word concerning my children. The moment I did that, His peace just rose up on the inside of me and came out of me and over me, as if someone had wrapped me in a warm blanket. I was aware of His presence and peace. My emotions immediately calmed, and I could think clearly. As Buddy prayed in the Spirit, the same thing happened to him, and he became peaceful.

First, my husband and I prayed in the Spirit so that we could restore His peace to our minds and emotions. Once we were calm and peaceful, we could pray some more and receive instruction on how to handle the situation when our child finally arrived home.

As we prayed, in this time in peace the Lord showed my husband exactly what had been going on, and He assured us that our child would be home soon. Not long after that, we heard the outside door open. The child was trying to enter the house quietly, hoping we were asleep. That hope was dashed as Buddy opened our bedroom door and said, "You need to come in here, please."

Buddy calmly said, "I can see that you are trying to think up something. Before you lie, let me tell you where you were, what you were doing, and why you are late."

Because my husband and I did not allow our emotions (the fleshly, carnal man) to rule, we were able to handle the situation and the necessary discipline by the wisdom of God, which produced peace in our home and in our children's lives. Had we allowed our emotions to rule, which is very easy for parents to do, we could have made the situation worse and harmed our relationship with our child and possibly the child's relationship with the Lord.

The Lord gives his people strength. The Lord blesses them with peace (Psalm 29:11 NLT).

The next morning, we sat down with all our children, reviewed the situation, and explained how we had prayed and trusted in the Lord. That circumstance became a testimony to our children of God's love, care, and capabilities. They realized that the Holy Ghost would "tell on them." Because Buddy and I chose to follow after peace, we prayed and trusted God. Then we chose to obey His instructions.

The choices we make will decide whether or not we have peace. Will we receive this gift from God and fight to maintain it, or will we become victims of circumstance?

As we walk in the presence and promises of Jesus, His peace permanently abides in us. He is our quietness, rest, and tranquility of heart and mind. Jesus' peace is not the absence of trouble. His peace is His presence in the midst of turmoil and trouble when our circumstances, minds, or lives seem out of control.

> *Peace I leave with you; My [own] peace I now give and bequeath to you. Not as the world gives do I give to you. Do not let your hearts be troubled, neither let them be afraid* (John 14:27 AMPC).

Notice that peace is the first word that Jesus says in this verse and it's also the subject of the sentence. Therefore, He is placing the emphasis on peace. If we read this in context, we realize that Jesus is preparing His disciples for what is yet to come: His betrayal and crucifixion. He wanted to assure His disciples that in the midst of trials they could have peace.

Also, notice one other thing Jesus told them in that verse: "Do not let your hearts be troubled and do not be afraid." Jesus was warning them to refuse the anxiety and fear. Maintaining His peace was their responsibility, even in the midst of trouble.

"*Thou wilt keep him in perfect peace, whose mind is stayed on thee; because he trusteth in thee*" (Isaiah 26:3 KJV). The New Revised Standard Version translates that passage, "*Those of steadfast mind you keep in peace, in peace because they trust in you.*" One commentary explained Isaiah 26:3 this way, "In the midst of difficulties and stress, God will keep those in true peace and spiritual well-being whose minds (including thoughts, impulses, and tendencies) are unshakeable and undeviating because they trust in God." *The World Bible Commentary* writes Isaiah 26:3 this way: "from a dependent attitude You form peace, peace when one's confidence (is) in You (God)."

To walk in Jesus' peace requires us to focus all of our thoughts, impulses, and tendencies on Him. We have to be totally dependent on Him.

A dependent attitude speaks of a willing and teachable heart, not a willful or rebellious one. It is a prerequisite for someone who is trusting God. If we are going to trust God, we have to depend on Him. If we are going to depend on God, we have to trust Him. Trust and dependence are the key ingredients to peace.

"*And the peace of God, which transcends all understanding, will guard your hearts and your minds in Christ Jesus*" (Philippians 4:7 NIV). The Rotherham Bible translates that verse this way: "*And, the peace of God, which riseth above every mind,*" and another translation (TCNT) reads, "*which surpasses every human conception.*" The God to whom we pray and offer thanksgiving, whose ways are higher than ours, is totally trustworthy. His peace accompanies our prayers and comes because prayer is an expression of trust. We do not need to have life all figured out in order to trust Him. We trust Him because we can't figure things out and He's the only one who has perfect knowledge. We must willingly surrender everything to Him and refuse to pick up what we have turned over to Him. Then the peace of God will work in our lives.

Sustaining peace is based on a consistent hope in and understanding of the promises of God. When we set our eyes on other things, we lose focus, hope, and peace. The apostle Paul told the Colossians, "*Set your mind on things above, not on things on the earth*" (Colossians 3:2 NKJV). I love how *The Message* translates that verse: "*Don't shuffle along, eyes to the ground, absorbed with the things right in front of you. Look up, and be alert to what is going on around Christ—that's where the action is. See things from his perspective.*" We are not to ignore circumstances and pretend they don't exist. Instead, we are to see them from Jesus' point of view.

Our job is to focus on Jesus, the Living Word of God, and point others to Him. Circumstances are temporal; they are subject to change at any moment. Only God and His Word are eternal and unchanging. We cannot depend on circumstances to give us lasting peace.

Turn away from evil and do good. Search for peace, and work to maintain it (Psalm 34:14 NLT).

Sustaining peace can only be found in the presence of the eternal, unchanging God Almighty. He wants us to have it.

So God has given both his promise and his oath. These two things are unchangeable because it is impossible for God to lie. Therefore, we who have fled to him for refuge can have great confidence as we hold to the hope that lies before us (Hebrews 6:18 NLT).

The two unchangeable things are the promises of God (for it is impossible for God to lie) and the oath by which God's promise is confirmed. Our hope and sustained peace is fixed after the eternal order of God. In God's order, His promises are made in perpetuity to His people. They have been secured for believers by Jesus Christ.

How often in difficult times have we heard someone say, *I need hope. I feel unsettled. So much is going on. What will happen, if...?* How many times have we surrendered our peace to "if"? John Calvin, the reformist of the early sixteenth century, wrote, "As the anchor joins the vessel with the earth, so the truth of God is a bond that connects us with Him. Thus when united to God, though we struggle with storms, we are still beyond the peril of shipwreck."

"*Thy word is a lamp unto my feet, and a light unto my path*" (Psalm 119:105 KJV). The Ferrar Fenton Bible reads, "*lights my steps, and enlightens my paths.*" The Bible in Basic English says, "*ever shining on my way.*" The psalmist makes an excellent point in this verse. A lamp is used at night; a light (sun) shines in the day. The Word covers both situations. We must always focus on God's truth when our paths are uncertain. The Word will show us the way. We love to have formulas for solving our problems: "six steps to," or "twelve steps to." But when our peace is threatened, our focus is blurred, and we forget those six or twelve steps, the Word will always light our paths.

In times of uncertainty, we need to rely on God's truth. The Word we read last year will not sustain us in a current trial or storm. Just as we need to walk life's path daily, we must also be shining or applying the light of God's Word to that path every day. That light, God's Word in the darkness of uncertainty, is the light for our feet—a sure direction for our next steps.

Why do we need God's light if we have natural light? The Word is the clarifying presence of God in every decision we make. We must base our decisions totally on His Word, which leads us and directs our thoughts to Him. When we walk in the light, we will be directed by His Word, drawn into His presence, sustained by His peace, and filled with His hope. The storms of life may come, but we will have sustaining peace because we are anchored to an immoveable object—the throne of God. We will be held fast by His presence, His peace, and His Word.

But seek first the kingdom of God and His righteousness, and all these things shall be added to you (Matthew 6:33 NKJV).

Chapter 5

MAINTAINING PEACE

In order to overcome in every area of our lives and maintain peace of heart and mind, we have to do something. We must make up our minds that we are going to overcome every attack or trick of the devil. We must make up our minds that the devil is not going to run over us. We cannot let the devil harass, pressure, torment, or cause us to be full of anxiety.

Peace or "unpeace" come down to a choice: Believe Jesus and His Word, or believe the devil and his lies. We choose whether to stay in Jesus' peace or open the door to "unpeace."

When I opened the door to "unpeace," I got into a place of depression. I didn't recognize what it was at first because I had never experienced it before. I didn't know what was happening to me. I had opened the door to depression because of my foolishness in taking offense, and I told God, *Well, if that's the way Your people are, I don't need to be in ministry. I quit.*

Because I took offense and got a wrong attitude, I opened the door for the enemy and lost my peace. I quit ministering. In my mind, I was in hell.

Many times, a good day for me was to get out of bed, walk across the bedroom floor, and sit down in the chair that was closest to me in the room. That was a *good* day. But was that peace? No, of course not!

I knew that God loved me and I loved Him more than anything in my life. His love brought me out of depression, and as I began to come out, there was peace. Boldness also came with this peace. It didn't matter what man or the devil said, I was not going to allow anyone or anything ever again to rob me of my peace. I was determined to maintain my peace and joy then, and I am just as determined now to maintain my peace and joy.

Since then I have had many opportunities to walk in unrest and "unpeace." But that day when I came out of depression and made my decision to obey the Lord and maintain my peace, I came out with a boldness that declared it didn't matter if people did not understand or receive my ministry gift. Because God gave me my gift, no man, devil, or anything else is going to keep me from ministering the way the Lord called me to minister. Now when I stand in the boldness of the anointing of the Holy Spirit,

I intend to do and say exactly what He says—*nothing more* and *nothing less.*

Every day I choose to maintain my peace, and you can maintain peace in every area of your life too. You just have to decide that you've had enough "unpeace" and discipline yourself to maintain His peace. You need to do this on a daily basis.

> *I listen carefully to what God the Lord is saying, for he speaks peace to his faithful people* (Psalm 85:8 NLT).

You discipline yourself to maintain His peace by making time each day to meet with the Lord. I know that may seem impossible because of all the demands on your time. but you don't have to start out with thirty minutes or even an hour. Maybe you can only take five or ten minutes a day to sit quietly before the Lord and let Him love on you. The important thing is to make time in your day for being with Jesus so that you can experience His love and peace.

The mind goes into neutral when we sit quietly and begin to pray in the Spirit. As we pray in the Spirit and speak forth the praises of God, our spirit man begins to rise up and the Holy Spirit begins to rise within us. We begin to confess scriptures that bring peace to us, so that when we get up from that time with the Lord, we are in peace.

The devil will bombard us with thoughts that we have no business thinking. Our minds will be running so fast that we can't think or make sense of what is what. Then we get frustrated. But God wants us to maintain peace. "*But seek first his kingdom and his righteousness*" (Matthew 6:33 NIV).

That's why we must pray in the Spirit (pray in tongues). Our recreated spirits know and understand God and His Word, but our minds and bodies don't. We have to do something to bring them in line with the Word of God and the spirit man. God created our bodies to function perfectly normal without any interruptions, foreign objects, or anything else.

I thank God every day that I am full of the life of God and the Holy Spirit. Therefore, I have the spirit of might that fills me through and through—every cell, bone, joint, vessel, artery—everything! There is no room or place for anything in my body that God did not create. This means that everything in my body must function as He created it to function and for the purpose He created it for.

If something is out of kilter, we have to put God's Word in our minds.

God will lead us to that knowledge, whether natural or spiritual. He will bring us to that knowledge and we can begin to walk in it.

As Christians, we get so busy helping others or working in the church that we don't help ourselves. I am not saying that we should not help others or work in the church. We just need balance in our lives. But if we are too busy helping others or working in the church so that we don't have any time to be with Jesus, then we are not going to be any good to anybody. We will not be as effective as we should be because we are doing life in our own strength rather than being led by the Holy Spirit. It is in those quiet times with Jesus, as we pray and read the Word, that we become aware of His presence, peace, and power. Then the Holy Spirit can show us how to face the day and how to handle whatever comes that day because we have taken the time to practice His presence and power.

You have to recognize that the enemy comes to your mind to get you in unpeace. If he can get you to accept his lie, you will move out of peace. Why do we so easily accept what the devil is saying when the Word of God plainly tells us that he is a liar, the father of lies, and there's no truth in him? We receive his lies and take hold of them hook, line, and sinker. Why?

Because we don't do what we need to do in our minds with the Word of God—always speaking forth the truth.

We should rise up and say to the devil, *Ha, devil, I got your number. That lying symptom is not part of me; I don't receive it. You can come no further. I'm full of the life of God, spirit of might. Besides that, I have the blood of Jesus as my protection and there is a bloodline around me that evil cannot penetrate through.* We have to talk to ourselves that way.

All the fruit of the Spirit work together. They are all interlocking. You really can't have one, in the fullness of the effect that is expected, without the other ones. I've seen this time and time again. I've seen it in my own life. Patience is the hardest one for me. Why? Because of the world we live in. Everything is instant. If it takes more than two minutes, it's too long!

We say, *I'm in a hurry; I'm in a hurry, God.* And what does He say? He says that one day is as a thousand years to Him.

We have allowed ourselves to believe we are earthly beings learning about God or learning about the things of God, because of the world's way of thinking. But that is not what the Bible says. The Word of God says that we are spiritual beings, aliens in the earth, and that this place is not our home. We were not born of this earth. The real man, our spirit man, was created by God. And since our Lord is in heaven, we are just pilgrims, or aliens, temporarily residing on earth with a plan and purpose given to us by God.

How do you think the devil came up with all these counterfeits about aliens and all this stuff? How do you think he gets that? He has no creativity. He draws it from God and the things of God and counterfeits it. The world may say, *Oh, there are these aliens coming from another planet and they look so weird and they're here for a purpose and this is their plan to destroy you.* This is totally opposite of the true plan of the real aliens here on this earth. Believers are aliens here on earth because our home is in heaven. And God has blessed us so that we can be a blessing to earth.

Our understanding, knowledge, and everything that we are and have is from God. We are not of this earth; we are of God who is in heaven. Therefore, He has given us an earth suit, which is our body, to live in while we are on the earth—to carry out His purpose and plan.

In the beginning, He made man perfect. When Jesus came and bought back everything from the devil that he had stolen, it was all restored to us.

So we can have God's best. We can have His peace, power, and presence every day, but we must read the Word and take hold of His promises for ourselves and walk in them every day. We can always operate in Jesus' peace by abiding in Him, seeking His kingdom, and allowing the fruit of the Spirit to be cultivated in us. Then we will have fruit that remains—one of which is peace.

> **Look at those who are honest and good, for a wonderful future awaits those who love peace (Psalm 37:37 NLT).**

Since we already have the peace of God, we must learn to cultivate it and stir it up within us.

> *Peace I leave with you; My [own] peace I now give and bequeath to you. Not as the world gives do I give to you. Do not let your hearts be troubled, neither let them be afraid. [Stop allowing yourselves*

to be agitated and disturbed; and do not permit yourselves to be fearful and intimidated and cowardly and unsettled] (John 14:27 AMPC).

I love this scripture because it shows me how much my Father God loves me. I can tell you, it's a reality to me because I've been there and I have experienced it firsthand. If peace isn't reigning in your heart and mind, you need to start letting those scriptures run over and over on the inside of you. Read them, speak them out loud, and meditate on them so the peace of God will come *on* you, *in* you, *through* you, *over* you, and *all around* you.

But seek first the kingdom of God and His righteousness, and all these things shall be added to you (Matthew 6:33 NKJV).

When we see something in our lives that starts leading us down a wrong path, we should stop it. We need to get back in line with the Word of God and the Spirit of God, so we can maintain the righteousness, peace, and joy that He has given us. But sometimes we don't do this. We just go headlong into the mess. Thank God He's merciful. Thank God for His grace and mercy. Thank God it's new every morning. We would all be in a mess if it wasn't, wouldn't we?

Even if we run headlong down this path knowing it's taking us the wrong way, He will send His angels to protect us and get us to the point where we can hear the Spirit of God and turn around and come back to what we know is true and right. Then peace and joy will come.

Peace I leave with you; My [own] peace I now give and bequeath to you. Not as the world gives do I give to you. Do not let your hearts be troubled, neither let them be afraid. [Stop allowing yourselves to be agitated and disturbed; and do not permit yourselves to be fearful and intimidated and cowardly and unsettled] (John 14:27 AMPC).

Jesus suffered on the cross and became the Prince of Peace. Since He lives on the inside of us, we have that peace. *You* have that peace. Notice that He says "peace I leave *with you.*" The word *you* is the understood subject of that sentence right? That's what Jesus said. He says *you,* because He is saying for *you* to stop allowing yourself to be agitated. *You* stop allowing yourself to be troubled. *You* stop allowing yourself to be afraid. *You* stop allowing yourself to be disturbed. He tells us not to permit ourselves to be fearful, intimidated, cowardly, or unsettled. *You* don't do it.

If He says that we can have peace, that means we can. That means when we do what He says according to the Word of God, we can stop "unpeace" from happening in our lives. Whether the attacks are coming against our minds, bodies, or circumstances, we can walk in peace and not allow ourselves to operate in fear, distress, intimidation, unrest or unpeace. But we have to do it. *You* have to do it!

One of our main problems is that a lot of times we don't want to do anything. We may say, *Well, God, I'm sitting here and You promised this or that.* But what are you doing to walk in that promise? Insecure people are afraid to make a decision. They are afraid to allow themselves to be what they know God wants them to be. They are afraid to allow people to see them as they really *are—human beings.*

Many times we are insecure because all of our thoughts are caught up in ourselves. *Well, I did this and I did that. And I don't want to do that. My this and my that.* It's all about us, what we are doing and what we can't do. God is saying that we are who we are because of Him, not because of what we have or haven't done.

We may look at people and think, *Oh, they are so perfect.* But nobody is perfect but Jesus. We need to stop and think. They are human beings just like we are. We are not supposed to compare ourselves to other people. We are supposed to find out from the Word of God who we are and what God has planned for us.

We need to get rid of insecurity, selfishness, and other negative things that we allow in our lives and move in closer to God. We need to have a relationship with Him, always maintaining our awareness of the righteousness, peace, and joy He has given us. We can demonstrate this by the Holy Spirit and by allowing God to be who He is in us and for us. We need to be who we are in Him instead of trying to be something else or someone else.

We need to be secure in God. He is the only one who makes us secure. We must choose to follow Him and walk in His truth. This will enable us to maintain our peace and joy. If we are in disobedience, the door is open and Satan has an entry point into our lives. The more we draw closer to God, have fellowship with Him, and get to know Him and not just His acts, the more we will know who we are and the more we will operate in the love of God. We will also experience the joy of the Lord, walk in righteousness, and maintain peace.

This is what God desires for us to walk in. He wants us to walk in the peace that He has already given us. He doesn't want us to let ourselves be troubled, agitated, fearful, intimidated, or walk down a wrong path because of things we have allowed to happen in our lives. He wants us to walk fully down the path He has designed for us, full of the love of God, operating in that love, and flowing in the joy of the Holy Ghost.

If we are going to keep Jesus' sayings and do them, we *cannot* allow ourselves to be agitated, fretful, intimidated, cowardly, or unsettled. We operate in the fullness of God by allowing the Holy Spirit to teach us about the things we have read in the Word of God and that God has said to us. At the time we need them, He will bring to our remembrance those things we have studied, that the Holy Spirit has helped us understand, and what the Holy Spirit has said.

> *Those who love your instructions have great peace and do not stumble* (Psalm 119:165 NLT).

Many times we don't see what God is doing because we are not developing our relationship with Him. We get caught up in the daily issues of life and allow the important things to take the place of the things that are vital. We need to understand and know the difference: God is life and that's vital to our lives. The important things that we have to deal with include food, clothing, transportation, and a roof over our heads. When we walk in the vitality of the life of God, the important things will be taken care of. We won't have to work hard to take care of the important things if we will take care of the vital first.

When we walk in fellowship with God and keep ourselves in line with the Word of God and the Spirit of God on a daily basis, we will be seeking God first and all the other things that are needful in our lives will come to us.

They will all be added to us. Quit trying to do life all by yourself. Walk in God and let God do it because He said He would. Then you will maintain peace. Jesus said that the way to refuse worry and to walk in peace is to "*seek first the kingdom of God and His righteousness, and all these things shall be added to you*" (Matthew 6:33 NKJV).

What's more important? Of course God is, because He's the one who is going to see that all the other things are added to you. You don't have faith in your faith. You have faith in God and His Word. Sometimes, we get so caught up in the workings of faith that we begin to have faith in our faith. Then we stumble and fall because we are not seeking His kingdom first and allowing Him to add all these things to our lives.

Do you know how you can tell when you are at the place where you are not seeking God first and allowing Him to add to you? You are anxious and impatient. You may say, *I asked for this a week ago and it's not here yet. What's going on?* God always answers prayer, but we must learn that He answers prayer according to His timing, plan, and purpose. A lot of times, the answer is right at our doorsteps ready to walk in and we say, *I don't know what's going on.* Impatient talk begins to come out of our mouths. Then, what we asked God for and He is sending stays outside the door because of our mouths. We block God's blessings in our lives, the answers to our prayers, because we aren't waiting in faith and peace with patience and love.

We need to make the decision that we will be disciplined and determined to do what God is saying to us. Then we will maintain peace in our hearts and minds. We can do this if we follow God on a daily basis and listen to the Holy Spirit. Did you know that God has every day planned for you? But you have to seek Him on a daily basis. How many of us do that? How many of us say, *God, here I am. I know that You have the designs of my life and You have designed this day that I am to abide in and walk in, and I'm listening to Your Holy Spirit to walk in that way.* When we do this, we maintain peace in our hearts and minds. God wants us to come into His peace.

> But now the Lord my God has given me peace on every side; I have no enemies, and all is well (1 Kings 5:4 NLT).

In order to fulfill what God has called us to do and bring others around us into the kingdom of God, we need to allow the love of God to work in us. We must walk in righteousness and maintain peace and joy to draw others to Him. No matter what happens, we should always have a *smile* on our faces. No matter what happens, we should always have joy. No matter what happens, we should always maintain *peace*. We are not going to draw others to Jesus by being impatient, out of peace, walking in unrighteousness, double-minded, up and down, having a frown on our faces, or by looking defeated.

People will not be drawn to Jesus if they don't see Him first in us. I don't know about you, but I want people to see the real me when they look at me. I don't want them to just see Pat Harrison, the human being. I want them to see the love of God. I want them to see the peace of God. I want them to see the joy of the Holy Ghost. I want them to see righteousness.

That should be the desire of our hearts.

But He was wounded for our transgressions, He was bruised for our guilt and iniquities; the chastisement [needful to obtain] peace and well-being for us was upon Him, and with the stripes [that wounded] Him we are healed and made whole (Isaiah 53:5 AMPC).

Chapter 6

CHASTISEMENT

When speaking of the Suffering Servant, Isaiah prophesied that Jesus bore our griefs, sorrows, pains, and punishment. Jesus didn't suffer *with* us; He suffered *for* us. Jesus wasn't sinful, sick, or distressed. We are. We need a savior. We need healing for our spirits, souls, and bodies.

Jesus already had peace with God. We humans are the ones who need reconciliation and peace with God. Therefore, Jesus suffered for us the punishment that rightfully belonged to us so that we can have the relationship with the Father that He has and all the blessings that go along with that relationship.

God made peace by the blood of the cross. Think about all that happened to Jesus: how He was beaten and spit upon, how spikes were nailed in His hands, and how a spear was driven into His side. He suffered all of the pain and humiliation so He could become peace for us. We can quote these verses from Isaiah, but do we ever think about what they really mean? What does the phrase *"chastisement [needful to obtain] peace and well-being for us was upon Him"* mean for us?

Chastisement means "the inflicting of pain to obtain peace." The infliction of pain to obtain peace was upon Jesus. Sin brought disorder, unpeace, into life and disrupted humanity's relationship with the Father God. In our sinfulness, we can never satisfy the demand of justice needed to pay the penalty for sin. But Jesus, the perfect and sinless one, could. He bore the punishment for us. He bore the sorrow. He bore the anxiety. He bore the pressure. He bore the trouble. He bore the tension and self-pity. He bore the mental anguish. He bore all those bad things so we don't have to.

Jesus bore everything our minds can conceive that would rob us of peace. He bore the punishment for sin in His mind as well as in His body. Therefore, if our minds are in a state of unrest, unpeace, or unease, we are not fully tapping into Jesus and who He is. He obtained perfect peace for us, so our minds can be in a state of tranquility and peace at all times. But we have to do something. We can't just sit back and let our minds wander in every direction.

We must take a good look at what Jesus has done for us and renew our minds. We must read and study the Word of God. We have to pray over that Word and ask the Holy Spirit to show us exactly what the Word means for us personally. We cannot settle for anything less than the total peace of God.

His government and its peace will never end. He will rule with fairness and justice from the throne of his ancestor David for all eternity. The passionate commitment of the Lord of Heaven's Armies will make this happen! (Isaiah 9:7 NLT)

We need to sense His peace from the tops of our heads to the tips of our toes—everywhere we go and in everything we do.

We don't have to be frustrated or in a state of unrest. Jesus was our substitute in everything. He took our place. We need to close our eyes and get a picture of Jesus' suffering for us, because He already suffered everything for us.

We cannot allow our minds to be in anguish and so mentally tormented that we cannot hear what the Spirit of God is saying to us. We don't have to walk around in agony of mind because Jesus came as the Prince of Peace.

Isaiah prophesied of the agony that Jesus would suffer for us. Isaiah 52:14 (NLT) says, *"But many were amazed when they saw him. His face was so disfigured he seemed hardly human, and from his appearance, one would scarcely know he was a man."*

The Bible says Jesus was unrecognizable. He was spit upon and beaten by the Sanhedrin before He was turned over to the Romans (see Matthew 26:67). He had on a crown of thorns, which punctured His head and caused blood to run down His face. He was scourged by the Romans, but that wouldn't cause Him to be unrecognizable. What caused Him to be unrecognizable? The torment He experienced in His mind caused Him to be unrecognizable.

Many times we think that He was unrecognizable just because of the physical suffering in His body. Yes, He suffered physically, but He also suffered mentally. On the cross, Jesus suffered in His mind. Why? Because the mind is the main battlefield of the devil.

Even though the scripture doesn't specifically say that Jesus suffered in His mind, it is apparent that He did because the scripture says He was unrecognizable. If you have ever worked or been around someone who has suffered mentally, you probably noticed that he or she does not look like himself or herself. This is because of the agony, pain, and mental anguish they experience. Jesus was unrecognizable because He was suffering all this mental anguish for us so we wouldn't have to. He did it for us!

When the enemy tries to come in our minds, we need to think about Jesus on the cross. We need to close our eyes and see Him suffering all that mental anguish for us. He was in such a state of unrest and unease in His mind that there was horrible anguish. He looked horrible and was unrecognizable because of the anguish and pain that He was suffering in His mind.

He bore that mental anguish and pain for us, so there's no need for us to bear it. To maintain peace we need to say, *No, I don't receive this mental torment. Jesus suffered that, so I don't have to. I'm going to remain in peace from the top of my head to the tips of my toes.* We have to be determined to do this daily until the peace and rest comes.

The devil brings torment through our minds. That's why we need to see Jesus at the point of wanting to pull His hair out because of all He was suffering. We need to see Jesus at the point where He is saying, *I can't take this pressure anymore.* We need to see Him at the point that He is so full of grief that a pity party wants to come on Him and His mind. He suffered all that. That's why He was not recognizable.

Have you ever seen someone who was so tormented in his mind that he became mentally ill? He didn't look like himself. If he were in an institution and you went to see him and pray with him, you would have noticed how different he looked. Why? Because of the anguish and the torment he was experiencing. Jesus suffered all of this so we can have peace. He suffered so we can have tranquility of mind.

Thou wilt keep him in perfect peace, whose mind is stayed on thee: because he trusteth in thee (Isaiah 26:3 KJV).

Let's say that unrest and distress are trying to come upon you because your spouse may not be doing things that are right in a marriage or covenant relationship. What should you do? You should not become agitated and let your mind run fifteen different directions. You should bring yourself back in line with the Word of God and bring peace to your mind. God is your source. God is the one who changes things, not you. God is the one who changes people, not you. If we could, we would change ourselves. But we certainly don't, do we? It takes God to work things out for our good.

We need God in every area of our lives. Every day we need to focus on Jesus. When we find ourselves in unpeace, we need to stop and just close our eyes and picture Him on the cross, unrecognizable because of the horrible torment that was happening in His mind for us. We need to go to the Word of God and find those scriptures on peace and how He bore our penalties and sin and suffered for us on the cross. Then we will be free and in total peace. We will be complete in Him—spirit, soul, and body.

When my husband, Buddy, decided to move to heaven, that was very difficult in many ways. I knew he was going, but letting go is never easy. Throughout our married life, we had done everything together. Besides our family, we were in ministry and business together. After Buddy went to heaven, I wasn't lonely because I have an intimate relationship with my Father God, Jesus, and the Holy Spirit, but I had to adjust to the difference of not having Buddy to talk with.

I can remember sitting in a business meeting, after Buddy was gone, and thinking, *Someone needs to say something. Why doesn't someone say something?* Then I realized that everyone was waiting on me to say something. After all, I was the boss. It was my job now to say something.

Since Buddy wasn't there to do it anymore, it was now my job to speak up.

At that time, the number of decisions that I needed to make and the amount of pressure upon me was almost overwhelming. I had to fight for my peace and rest. I sought the Lord, but I didn't beg Him for help because that's not faith. I had to pray with my understanding and in the Spirit so that my natural man would calm down. Once I was calm, the spirit man could rise up and I could hear what the Lord was saying to me.

During that time of transition when Buddy went to heaven, the Lord told me to continually meditate on two scriptures: Isaiah 26:3 and Psalm 34:7. All day long I would think on those verses. I would say them out loud. I would pray them out loud. I would thank God that my mind and emotions were in perfect peace because I was trusting in Him and keeping my focus on Him. I would praise God that His angels were stationed all around me to deliver me from every wicked and evil scheme.

I would praise Jesus for all He did for me when He suffered and died on the cross. I would picture Jesus taking upon Himself all the torment, fear, and distress that was trying to come on me. And I refused to receive torment, fear, and distress because He already took them for me. That is how I walked through those difficult days in peace.

The Angel of the Lord encamps around those who fear Him [who revere and worship Him with awe] and each of them He delivers (Psalm 34:7 AMPC).

The process of walking and living in peace starts with understanding that the chastisement, the punishment, that Jesus suffered healed us in every way—spirit, soul, and body.

We will never be whole if our souls are not healed. Operating in peace is part of the healing process for the soul. Isaiah 53:5 (NKJV) says, "*But He was wounded for our transgressions, He was bruised for our iniquities; the chastisement for our peace was upon Him, and by His stripes we are healed.*" The chastisement needful to obtain peace and wellbeing for us was placed upon Jesus. A lot of times, we think that healing is only for the body, but it's also for the soul and mind. Jesus bore stripes for the healing of our bodies. And He also bore agony of mind for the healing of our souls.

When the Word of God says that there is nothing we can be involved with or any circumstance that will come against us that Christ cannot identify with, that means *everything*. It means that He had to suffer mentally in His mind. Unrest and unpeace begin in the mind.

We have to understand that Jesus suffered that agony in His mind and spirit so that we can have peace, quietness, and rest.

We don't have to buy into the lies of the devil because Jesus obtained peace for us. Our minds can be in a state of tranquility and peace at all times, just as the spirit man is. We should not settle for anything less than the peace of God totally saturating us.

Jesus did it for us; therefore, we can operate in peace. We need to understand what He has done for us. When we get to the place that we are frustrated or feel like we want to pull our hair out, we need to see Jesus on the cross suffering for us, knowing that He has already born the torrent so that we don't have to. We need to say, *Satan, you're not going to rob my peace. I'm going to stay in the presence of the Lord Jesus Christ and maintain my peace, because He bought it for me. He is the Prince of Peace. Therefore, He is my peace. Hallelujah.*

And I will pray the Father, and he shall give you another Comforter, that he may abide with you for ever (John 14:16 KJV).

Chapter 7

COMFORTABLE OR CONTENTED

Oftentimes, people think that all their problems in life are over when they get saved. From now on, life should be comfortable and carefree, right? Wrong! That is not scriptural. Life doesn't become comfortable and problem-free because one said the sinner's prayer. In

John 16:33 (KJV) Jesus said, "*These things I have spoken unto you, that in me ye might have peace. In the world ye shall have tribulation: but be of good cheer; I have overcome the world.*"

Yes, we will encounter challenges and hard times as long as we live in this world, but that doesn't mean that we should be sad, distressed, or defeated. We can overcome because Jesus overcame for us.

Jesus promised that we would have help in this life. Since He was returning to heaven, He would send Someone just like Himself: "*And I will pray the Father, and he shall give you another Comforter, that he may abide with you for ever*" (John 14:16 KJV).

Because of the modern meaning of the word *comforter*, we think that the Holy Spirit is here to empathize with us, hold our hands, and speak soothing words as we go through difficult times. But that is not an accurate picture of the Holy Spirit. He does more than assure us. He provides assistance and strengthens us so that we overcome. He brings truth to our minds and keeps us on the right course. He reminds us of what Jesus said and empowers us to keep His commands. The Holy Spirit isn't going to make life comfortable for us. He will empower us to overcome—if we allow Him to do so.

I have had a lot of uncomfortable days in my life. For starters, I was a very shy and introverted person. I would rather sit on the back row, stay out of the limelight, and never say a word. But that isn't what God had planned for me. I had to rely on the Holy Spirit to empower me so that I could minister.

When I began to study on the subject of love, the Holy Spirit instructed me to confess 1 Corinthians 13:4-8. Everywhere the word *love* was used, I was to say, "I am." For example, verse 4 (NKJV) says, *"Love suffers long and is kind; love does not envy; love does not parade itself, is not puffed up."* I had to confess, "I suffer long and am kind. I am not envious. I do not parade myself and I am not puffed up." That was uncomfortable! For the longest time, it felt as if I were lying.

I have told you these things, so that in Me you may have [perfect] peace and confidence. In the world you have tribulation and trials and distress and frustration; but be of good cheer [take courage; be confident, certain, undaunted]! For I have overcome the world. [I have deprived it of power to harm you and have conquered it for you] (John 16:33 AMPC).

It wasn't comfortable or pleasant when my husband Buddy decided to move to heaven. Since the day we married, we had been a team.

Together we made decisions about the family, the businesses, and the ministry. Now, half of the team was in heaven. This was a huge change, and I had a lot of decisions to make without him. But because I knew the Holy Spirit and I knew how to stay in the peace of God, I came through that transition victoriously.

The Holy Spirit will do everything and be everything Jesus said—if we will allow Him to fulfill His ministry through us and be who He is in us. Though Jesus is no longer physically present on earth, the Holy Spirit is here to enable us to walk in all that the Word says is ours.

The peace that Jesus Christ has given to us comes from looking into His face through His Word, because He and His Word are one. Part of the Holy Spirit's ministry is to give us understanding of the Word and how to walk in it.

We need to fully understand and receive the contentment that comes from Him. We have to understand there's a difference between being contented and being comfortable.

Contentment causes us to be steadfast and to know that we know that we know what the Word of God says is true. Then we can operate and maintain everything that God has said in our lives: love, joy, peace, gentleness, forbearance, and patience. All these things produce contentment. In contentment, we will know God. We will be quick to obey the will of God. We will know that we can do what He says, not in the natural, but according to His abilities that He has given us and the gifts and graces He has placed on the inside of us.

On the other hand, being comfortable is allowing ourselves to get in a place where we don't want to be disturbed, don't want to make any changes, or do anything that is challenging. When we are in our own little comfort zones, we are comfortable with everything around us and it's so wonderful. We don't want God to ask us to do something hard or impossible that is going to require us to use our faith. We say, *Don't bother me; I'm doing real good right here. I want to stay right here. I'm just real comfortable.*

But being in a *comfort zone* is spiritually dangerous because we will depend upon our own abilities and do things our way rather than trusting in God and doing things His way. And we certainly don't want to do anything that would challenge our faith and make us uncomfortable. The things that He asks us to do cannot be accomplished in our own strength or by our abilities and talents. What good would it be for Him to ask us to do things that we can do for ourselves in the natural? We would never totally trust and lean on Him. We would continue to lean on ourselves and our own understanding.

Proverbs 3:5-8 (NKJV) says:

*Trust in the Lord with all your heart, and
lean not on your own understanding; in
all your ways acknowledge Him, and He
shall direct your paths. Do not be wise in
your own eyes; fear the Lord and depart
from evil. It will be health to your flesh,
and strength to your bones.*

The Hebrew word for *lean* means to support yourself. We are not to support ourselves independently of God. We are to depend on Him. He is the source of all supply, and that includes the supply of peace.

We are going to cause ourselves all kinds of problems when we forget to go to God and ask Him what to do. But if we want to stay in peace and contentment, we must go to the Lord first. *Jesus, I need help. Show me how to handle this. I am trusting You for wisdom and understanding. I choose to allow Your peace to keep me through this.* Then as we pray in the Holy Spirit and worship the Lord, His peace wells up inside us and overflows out of us. Then we can think clearly and hear His instructions.

> Submit to God, and you will have peace; then things will go well for you (Job 22:21 NLT).

We must keep our minds stayed on Him in order to remain in contentment and peace. "*May God give you more and more grace and peace as you grow in your knowledge of God and Jesus our Lord*" (2 Peter 1:2 NLT). Notice that Peter said peace is multiplied through the knowledge of God and Jesus. Peter was not talking about a knowledge that came from only reading a book. He was referring to a knowledge that came from a personal experience. What does that mean? It means that we must spend time with the Lord through prayer, worship, and study of the Word in order for peace to be multiplied in our lives. Nothing that God has promised will operate in our lives to its fullest when we are in unrest and unpeace.

The more we experience the Lord's presence and power, the more peace will be multiplied into our lives. When we get in unrest and unpeace, we are not quiet. Our minds are running in all these different directions, we're being bombarded with thoughts, and we are running here and there trying to keep up. We have to bring our minds back into control by the Word of God and the Spirit of God. Then we can remain in peace and contentment and continue to have that peace multiplied in our lives. We are responsible for taking control of our minds by God's Word and power. The apostle Paul wrote that the weapons of our warfare, which include prayer and the speaking of God's Word, enable us to cast down any wrong thought that is trying to exalt itself above the knowledge of God (see 2 Corinthians 10:5).

May God give you more and more grace and peace as you grow in your knowledge of God and Jesus our Lord (2 Peter 1:2 NLT).

Praying in the Spirit and speaking God's Word are more powerful than anything the devil throws at us.

Because Paul knew the power and victory that comes from knowing God, he prayed for believers:

> *For this reason we also, from the day we heard of it, have not ceased to pray and make [special] request for you, [asking] that you may be filled with the foil (deep and clear) knowledge of His will in all spiritual wisdom [in comprehensive insight into the ways and purposes of God] and in understanding and discernment of spiritual things* (Colossians 1:9 AMPC).

There are a lot of opportunities for us to get in unrest. What does God's Word say? He says that we have to be filled with the knowledge of Him and His Word. We know Him through His Word.

When we get into the wonderful Word of God, we will begin to imitate God. And God is peace. We will begin to think like He thinks. We will begin to walk like He walks. We will begin to talk like He talks. We will begin to act like He acts. This is the heart of God. This process is what the apostle Paul called "transformation."

And do not be conformed to this world, but be transformed by the renewing of your mind, that you may prove what is that good and acceptable and perfect will of God (Romans 12:2 NKJV).

Unless we renew our minds through the Word and prayer, we will not be able to maintain this peace in our minds. We will begin to think and look in every direction except where we need to. A renewed mind will enable us to see life—truth—from God's perspective. Thus we will have peace and contentment, even in the midst of uncomfortable circumstances.

Jesus and the Word are one. He is the Word made flesh (see John 1:1). He only speaks and knows what the Father speaks and knows. Likewise, we should also only speak and know what the Father speaks and knows. Then we will remain in peace and fulfill what God has called us to do. He has called us for a specific plan and purpose, individually and as a body.

Many times we stay in our comfort zones and don't rock the boat or change anything. Why? Because of fear. When we are not in peace, there is going to be fear. But you know what? When we truly walk in God's plan and the destiny He has for our lives, we will seek to know His will.

The hardest change to make is the one on the inside of us because we want to hold on to things. Some things we should hold on to, but holding on to the wrong things will hinder us from all that God has for us. He wants us to change into His image. Many times, however, we don't want to do it God's way, even though we have said, *God, my heart is Your heart. I want Your will to be my will.* Then when He starts working in us, we decide we don't want it.

We have to keep our minds in line with the Word of God so that we don't get in unrest and unpeace. We need to stay in peace so that we can clearly hear what God says and operate and go forth in the destiny that He has planned for us. God has a destiny for each one of us, but it's up to us to follow it through and fulfill it in our lives.

Conformity to what the world says is low-risk living. We want to be safe and feel safe. The world supposedly gives us all the things we need to make us safe and feel safe, but it never happens. Why? Because there's only one source of security—God. He tells us we can change something, but we need to let Him operate that change and believe Him enough to know that we can do what He says because we have His complete help.

Sometimes we find ourselves held in a *paradigm*. A paradigm is a specific way of looking at something. In other words, we have a set way of looking at things and we don't want to shift or change. But we have to shift that paradigm that got us set in a rut, so to speak, until we shift our habits and patterns to line up with what God says He wants for our lives.

The reason we don't do this and keep moving and shifting our habits and patterns is because we are so strong-willed and hard-headed. We say, *But God, I like this and I want this, and look what's happened with me doing this.* And God is saying, *You need to shift; you need to move. There's nothing wrong with that and what's happened is wonderful and good, but I'm trying to move you further so more things can happen. It will be more dynamic in your life.*

I want God to be dynamic in my life. When people see me, I want them to see joy, love, peace, and righteousness. Even though the world doesn't realize it, that's what they hunger for. That's what they are seeking. We need to shift our habits and patterns to line up with what God wants for our lives.

We need to change the way we think about things and do something about it. And what's that? We need to obey God, walk in obedience to what He says, and allow our habits to be changed. We are in the habit of washing our faces, brushing our teeth, taking a shower, and having a cup of coffee. There's nothing wrong with any of these things. They are habits—we don't have to think about them.

God wants to change our habits because He wants us to look at Him and know that He is the way of life. We must grow in Him because the more we grow, the more change comes. The more we grow, the more knowledge we have, and the more knowledge we have, the more responsibility we will also have.

This is where a lot of people get hung up. They don't want to be responsible for anything, even themselves. But God says we are responsible for ourselves. We are also responsible for others because He has called us into this world to pour ourselves out to a lost and dying world, so they can come into the saving knowledge of the Lord Jesus Christ.

Many of us operate in unpeace because we are not moving into what God has said. When we get just a little closer to God, we realize we have never led anyone to the Lord or even asked if they knew Jesus. We also realize that we have never even said a kind word to someone who is struggling with some type of addiction.

We get into condemnation and allow our minds to roam or wander.

As a result, we pull away from God instead of staying right there. We wander around in the wilderness for a while and think, *Well, I'm tired of this. This is dry; I don't like to be dry.* Then we move back in closer to God again. As we get closer to Him, change is mentioned and we move out again.

The natural man does not like change. Our minds like their little habits. However, when we come to know the Lord Jesus Christ, our thinking begins to change because of the spirit man within us. But our minds will fight us all the way. That's why we need to study the Word of God and begin to think the way God thinks.

The natural man does not want to change those habits. He doesn't want to change his wrong thinking. You can always tell what people have put into their minds by what comes out of their mouths. If they have their minds renewed with the Word of God and are in control, they will only speak what the Father speaks, but if they don't, they will speak what their bodies speak.

> *A good man out of the good treasure of his heart brings forth good; and an evil man out of the evil treasure of his heart brings forth evil. For out of the abundance of the heart his mouth speaks* (Luke 6:45 NKJV).

The body has a voice. The mind has a voice. The soul has a voice. And the spirit has a voice. Which one are you following? If you are not following the real you, the spirit man, you are either following the soul or the body, and you will be in unrest and unpeace.

In Genesis 12, God told Abraham to move to a different country. Abraham got up and moved because he loved God and knew that God would not fail him. Even though Abraham did not know where he was going, in faith he obeyed God's Word.

I will feed the poor in my pasture; the needy will lie down in peace (Isaiah 14:30 NLT).

We need to realize that even though we may not know where we are going when God asks us to change, we can't allow ourselves to be troubled. Abraham had no idea where he was going. You would think that he would have been concerned or troubled, but he wasn't. He didn't worry and mull over every little detail in his mind, wondering, *Well, what about this? What if I'm going in the wrong direction? I don't know where I'm going. What if I'm going around in circles?*

That's how our minds work. But Abraham did not trouble his mind with all that because he trusted God and by faith received his inheritance. Most of us want to receive the inheritance before we believe God. But we are not going to have our full inheritance until we walk out by faith the destiny in our lives that God has planned for us. Maintaining peace is part of this process.

There are things that God is going to call us to do that require change. We have to change. We must do what He says even though we have never done it before, in order to walk out the destiny God has for us. In other words, we are going to have to do something we have never done before.

That is why the Christian life is called a walk of faith. When God begins to move or change us level by level, step by step, there's always something we are going to have to do that we have never done before and that will make us uncomfortable. But through that change and in doing these things, we will be brought up to another level in God.

That's what He desires. He wants us to always be moving up instead of staying at a plateau or going backward. He wants us to move forward. Then we will experience peace even in the midst of changes in our lives, because He is moving us closer to our destiny.

As we follow Him, our destiny will be fulfilled by His Spirit and His Word. In Hebrews 11, there were instances where Isaac, Jacob, Joseph, and others acted by faith and obeyed God. They heard God speak to them about His plan for their lives, and they believed what He said and acted upon their belief.

If we take a closer look at the lives of these individuals, we will see that their obedience guarded their future. Their destiny was secured every step of the way as they heard, believed, and acted upon the Word of God for their lives.

We could even take this a step further and say that their faith even guarded *our* destiny.

We know that because of the trails that they blazed, we benefit from their lives today. Right? And they were people just like us. Sometimes we think the people who lived in Bible days were different from us. But people have been people for as long as God created them. They are the same. They are people.

Those in the Word of God who were given to us as examples were real people just like us. If we take heed to their mistakes and their successes, we will be blessed and helped by the Spirit of God as well.

They did not have easy lives. They certainly did not have the comforts that we have in this dispensation today. We have so many comforts; we want everything done for us. But if we are living by the Word of God, we must exercise our faith. We have to take hold and have the tenacity to say, *This is truth. I don't care what's true. This Word is truth and this is what I live in. This truth, no other truth. This is the truth I live in. I don't care who says what, what comes, what goes, this is truth. This is what I live in. God is my God, He's my Father God, and He will not fail me, He will not cause me to be cast down, but He will continually take me forward and upward in the destiny that He has called for my life.*

Sometimes we are tempted to feel sorry for ourselves. This happened in the Bible too. There were pity parties in the Bible. Sometimes we think that God has called us to do something that's not easy. But we need to realize that everything God calls us to do is not easy to our minds.

We tend to confuse our destiny with our salvation. Jesus came to die for us and purchase our salvation. Therefore, salvation is a free gift from God. However, our destiny costs us everything. But it is well worth it. The life we live is not our own; it's the life of Jesus Christ.

We gain something that no money can buy and no natural man on this earth today can give to us. We can give it to ourselves as a godly gift. This gift is everything we are and everything we have, while walking in the fullness and complete plan and purpose of God in our lives to fulfill our destiny.

Sometimes we have to work harder, fight harder, and pay more. But that's okay. Do you know why we have to do that? The devil wants to fight us every step of the way because he wants to make our lives and paths as confusing as possible. He doesn't want us to fulfill our destinies.

The devil knows that when we fulfill our destinies, we are just like Jesus, and he doesn't want us to be like Jesus. That's why he comes against us. It's not because of who we are, so don't take the devil's attacks personally. He is not interested in us; that's evident because he kills the people who live for him. If he were interested in people, he wouldn't kill those who were living for him and serving him, but he does.

He is interested in Jesus and the Jesus in us. He thinks if he can deter or defeat us, he will be one step closer to getting to Jesus. He doesn't have enough sense to know he has already been defeated and is never going to get to Jesus. That's why it's so interesting to me when people who call themselves Christians have more faith in the devil's power than they do in God's. They say, *Well, I saw what the devil did.* So what? I've seen what God has done and it's mightier than anything the devil has ever done.

Everything the devil does leads to death and destruction. And everything God does leads to life, love, joy, peace, and righteousness.

God has a path for us—our destiny. While walking in our destiny, He wants us to walk in perfect peace. There is a peace we can walk in when the storms of life are raging around us.

I know this because I personally experience it every day.

> *Lord, you will grant us peace; all we have accomplished is really from you* (Isaiah 26:12 NLT).

There is a peace that we can come to in God where it doesn't matter what's going on around us. All the negative things and storms that try to create havoc in our lives are lies of the devil, and the Word of God says that he is a liar and the father of lies:

> *You are of your father the devil, and the desires of your father you want to do. He was a murderer from the beginning, and does not stand in the truth, because there is no truth in him. When he speaks a lie, he speaks from his own resources, for he is a liar and the father of it* (John 8:44 NKJV).

What does that mean? That means there's no truth in him, so why believe him?

Our minds pick up everything the devil says and blow it out of proportion, because we think on it for so long that we no longer see God, what He is doing, and what He has said in our lives because we have this big picture of the ugly devil. But remember, he has been defeated. Jesus overcame him so we are more than overcomers in Christ Jesus.

We can have peace in the midst of a storm. We can fulfill our destiny and walk in His will, no matter what circumstances come our way or what is raging around us. Storms eventually subside. Where are you going to be when that storm subsides? Are you going to be on the other side or are you going to be shipwrecked, hurt, crippled, defeated, or feeling sorry for yourself?

Jesus says you can go to the other side in any storm, but you can't lose sight of where you are headed. You cannot lose sight of the destiny God has placed in your heart. One of the ways you can do this is by maintaining peace in your life. And if you don't exactly know where you are headed, just keep seeking God—stay on your knees, stay in the Word, stay open to God, and stay faithful to the priorities of life right where you are.

If you stay in peace and in God's plan, you will realize that your destiny is not for sale. You can put up a sign to Satan that says, *My destiny is not for sale. You can't buy me, Satan, no matter what you put up before me. They are all lies because you are a liar and the father of lies. There is no truth in you and, therefore, my destiny is not for sale. But I maintain and walk in the peace of God, and because I walk in that peace then my flesh stays in line with the Word of God. My mind stays in line with the Word of God, and I live in His peace In my life every day and I obey and I act on His Word and I will fulfill my destiny.*

Can you say with a pure heart that you will fulfill your destiny no matter what mistakes you have made? I pray that you have learned from your mistakes and go on from there. God didn't call us to sit by our mistakes. He called us to look at what has happened and look at the Word of God and move on.

He didn't call us to stay by our successes either. We can't say, *Look what I have done.* If we do, we will surely fall. He has called us to operate in His peace and to maintain that peace every day of our lives. We need to allow His peace to rise up within us, come out of our mouths, and cover and surround us as a protection to fulfill the destiny that God has called us to.

Did you know that as you seek the Lord and obey Him every day of your life, you are one step closer to your destiny? Why? Because you sought God and you obeyed exactly what He said to do. We can't wait to call on God when we are distraught or facing overwhelming circumstances. This has to be a way of life. Then what someone said or did won't rob you of your peace.

For He is [Himself] our peace (our bond of unity and harmony). He has made us both [Jew and Gentile] one [body], and has broken down (destroyed, abolished) the hostile dividing wall between us, by abolishing in His [own crucified] flesh the enmity [caused by] the Law with its decrees and ordinances [which He annulled]; that He from the two might create in Himself one new man [one new quality of humanity out of the two], so making peace (Ephesians 2:14-15 AMPC).

Chapter 8

THE WITNESS OF PEACE

When God first began to deal with me about moving out into a pulpit ministry, I was mortified because I was very shy, introverted, and easily intimidated by others. I know that's hard to believe, but it's true. My heart was to walk in the complete will of God. I wanted my will to be His will.

When you have these desires, it's hard to ignore what God is saying to you, but you still try. That's when you get to the place where you pray in the spirit but don't stop to listen. You know what He is going to say, but you don't want to hear it.

I said, *God, I can't do that. You know, even when I'm called on to give a short testimony or share something, I shake all over. I shake so bad, my voice shakes and everybody knows I'm frightened out of my wits. So what good is that going to do?* But God said to me, *You're looking at the wrong person.* Well, I knew exactly what He meant by that, so that was the end of that conversation. Over the years, I have learned that obedience is better than sacrifice.

When God began to move me into a pulpit ministry, it was a big change for me. In the past, I held prayer groups in my home and taught the women about prayer and the Holy Spirit. I loved doing that, but I never got up in the pulpit. Then

God said, *You need to. That's what I want you to do.* That meant that I had to allow the Holy Spirit to work in me and through me to get fear out of my life, because shyness and intimidation are byproducts of fear. I had to let go of all my fears and allow the Word of God to heal me and bring me into the fullness of what God had for my life.

Many years before I began teaching, God had me study the topic of love. For two years, I studied everything about God's love. I used to tease our congregation when we pioneered our first church, Faith Christian Fellowship. Of course they knew I loved them, but sometimes I would say things like, "You know, you're the reason that God had me in the love chapters and studying God's love for two years."

There was more truth to that than I realized at the time. It wasn't because of those people; it was so that I could understand the heart of God. That's who He is. First John 4:8 (NKJV) says, "*He who does not love does not know God, for God is love.*"

God wanted me to have the right kind of love for people. He wanted me to love people the way He loves people. The world's love is "performance-based" love. I had a lot to overcome, but thank God He put me in the right place to overcome it. I learned about Him and who He is. If I can do it, you can too!

Are you in complete obedience? Are you seeking Him daily to walk out His plan for your life? That's what's important. It's very important.

Even though we may know the love of God and how to pray in the Spirit, build ourselves up, listen to God, and hear what He is saying, we can still allow our minds to overtake us at times. When we do this, we allow ourselves to get in unrest or unpeace.

And this righteousness will bring peace. Yes, it will bring quietness and confidence forever (Isaiah 32:17 NLT).

God has called us to be people of peace. We are the only Jesus many people will ever see. The reason they are drawn to us is because they see the attributes of Jesus in us—joy and peace.

> *For He is [Himself] our peace (our bond of unity and harmony). He has made us both [Jew and Gentile] one [body], and has broken down (destroyed, abolished) the hostile dividing wall between us, by abolishing in His [own crucified] flesh the enmity [caused by] the Law with its decrees and ordinances [which He annulled]; that He from the two might create in Himself one new man [one new quality of*

humanity out of the two], so making peace
(Ephesians 2:14-15 AMPC).

We need to meditate on these scriptures and look at the different translations. God created one man, abolishing or annulling the law so there's one new quality of humanity. He made peace. Peace is here because Jesus made peace for us. He did it in His own body. Until Jesus came to earth, died, rose again, and was seated at the right side of His Father, this supernatural peace wasn't available

The kingdom of God is within us. Luke 17:21 (NKJV) says, "*Nor will they say, 'See here!' or 'See there!' For indeed, the kingdom of God is within you.*" Because Jesus is the King and we have received Him as our Lord and Savior, He lives in us. We cannot find peace in outward circumstances. So why are we looking out there for peace? Peace is right here on the inside of us. Jesus said, "If you receive me I come to abide with you. Not only that, I bring the Father and

He abides with you. And then I have left the Holy Spirit here on the earth for you, which is the Spirit of God who speaks forth that which God wills."

If we look through the Word, we will see that time and time again, God wills it, Jesus speaks it, and the Holy Spirit does it or demonstrates it in our lives. Because the kingdom of God is on the inside of us, we have righteousness, peace, and joy in the Holy Ghost (see 2 Thessalonians 3:16). In that scripture, He says we should have the peace of God surrounding us at all times. The reason we can't get into that flow of praying in the spirit, yielding ourselves to the Holy Spirit, and listening to what God is saying to us by His Holy Spirit is because we have not brought our minds into control. Our minds are running here and there, and when we finally get quiet we think, *Well, what's the use? I might as well get up because I can't control my mind. My mind's just running wild.*

Well, speak peace to it. Bring that peace into your mind. Just because you have a bunch of thoughts coming to your mind doesn't mean that you should receive them and think about them. You are responsible for taking authority over your mind.

When a thought of worry or fear comes, speak to it: "No, I don't receive you." You replace that negative thought with God's Word about your situation. For example, this thought comes, *I don't have the money to pay this bill,* and with it comes the emotion of fear. You speak to that thought: *Devil, you're a liar. I do not receive that thought. That bill is not my problem. God supplies all of my needs according to His riches in glory by Christ Jesus. My Father knows what I need, and He gives me everything I need for life and godliness.* Then you begin to praise and thank the Lord for taking care of you. Because you are speaking God's Word and praising Him, your mind is stayed on Him and you will experience His peace. Your peaceful presence witnesses to others and brings glory to God.

Jesus is the Prince of Peace. So if you bring peace to your mind, then you bring Jesus to your mind and it won't wander here and there. You will only have the thoughts of the Lord Jesus Christ and the Word of God. It may be through a revelation, an impression, a knowing, a prophecy, or a vision. It doesn't matter what form it comes in; it only matters that you take the time to listen. You cannot do this when your mind is in unpeace.

God created you, the body, your earth suit, as well as the spirit man. He set natural and spiritual laws into motion and they work together. The spirit man, the real you, has an understanding of all these natural and spiritual laws, but your mind does not. Your mind is not redeemed; therefore, you must renew it with the Word of God.

Finally, brethren, whatsoever things are true, whatsoever things are honest, whatsoever things are just, whatsoever things are pure, whatsoever things are lovely, whatsoever things are of good report; if there be any virtue, and if there be any praise, think on these things (Philippians 4:8 KJV).

We need to keep our mind on Jesus, and as we do the Holy Spirit will work all things in us, including God's peace.

Buddy used to talk about getting caught in the middle of the smack—when God kisses earth. That's what peace is—smack in the middle of God, regardless of the circumstances.

Isaiah 26:3 (KJV) says, "*Thou wilt keep him in perfect peace, whose mind is stayed on thee: because he trusteth in thee.*" Peace is essential in our lives. Our homes should be havens of peace. Keeping His peace in our homes and lives is very important. Peace is the green-house of miracles. The controlled environment of the greenhouse ensures that the plants grow and thrive.

Peace builds a shelter around us, enabling us to control our minds, emotions, and inner resources in order to bring about the desired results. As we remain peaceful, we can focus our faith on Him and His Word, expecting to receive what we need.

Peace is attainable because Jesus bought it at the cross. He told the disciples He was leaving His peace on earth. In a crisis, there is nothing more powerful than the calming presence of God. Seek God and find His peace. It can, and it will, sustain you in your life and ministry.

How do we seek God? We seek God by med-itating on His person—who Jesus is. God keeps the one whose mind is stayed or fixed on Him. We seek God by meditating on His presence. The Lord inhabits the praises of His people.

When we meditate on Him and His goodness, we can't help but praise Him for who He is and all that He has done. Another way we seek God is by meditating on His purpose. He has chosen us for good, not evil. When our minds are stayed on Him, we realize His purpose for our lives.

Peace brings strength. It provides shelter during the greatest storms of our lives. We need to let peace envelop us. In the refuge of His presence, we will find our joy. It isn't easy to remain in peace; it's work. It takes concentrated effort, but it's worth it.

Jesus brings us that peace, tranquility of heart and mind. Paul wrote:

> *For He is [Himself] our peace (our bond of unity and harmony). He has made us both [Jew and Gentile] one [body], and has broken down (destroyed, abolished) the hostile dividing wall between us, by abolishing in His [own crucified] flesh the*

enmity [caused by] the Law with its decrees and ordinances [which He annulled]; that He from the two might create in Himself one new man [one new quality of humanity out of the two], so making peace (Ephesians 2:14-15 AMPC).

Where is Jesus, the Prince of Peace? He is on the throne, but He is also in our hearts. He lives in us and we live in Him. If He is peace and the Prince of Peace, then we have peace because we have Him. Regardless of our circumstances, we have peace as long as we have Jesus. We can have tranquility of heart and mind because of Jesus.

To operate in faith, it is vital to have Jesus and His peace in our lives.

Oh, that you had listened to my commands! Then you would have had peace flowing like a gentle river and righteousness rolling over you like waves in the sea (Isaiah 48:18 NLT).

As long as we are in unpeace and unrest, our faith will not operate as it should. It will be wavering up and down. When we are in unpeace and unrest, we can't focus on the Word of God. Our minds and emotions will go crazy and we won't be able to hear His voice. On the other hand, when we are in peace and rest, then our faith is strong and we won't waver. We will see the manifestation of our faith; our faith will work.

> *But He was wounded for our transgressions, He was bruised for our guilt and iniquities; the chastisement [needful to obtain] peace and well-being for us was upon Him, and with the stripes [that wounded] Him we are healed and made whole* (Isaiah 53:5 AMPC).

We are not going to be made whole if we don't have peace. We need peace in order to receive our healing. Peace makes our faith operative.

Peace is an important part of our witness to the world. People who do not have peace are negative and unhappy. They are not operating in the love or joy of God. Since they are unhappy, they want everyone else to be unhappy too. Consequently, no one wants to be around them. But when we have peace and the joy of the Lord, we will have a spring in our step and a smile on our face. We will rejoice and walk in the love of God and people will want to know why we are so full of joy and peace, even in the midst of terrible conditions.

Not long after Buddy and I started our publishing company, a very difficult and potentially disastrous situation occurred. I was at home praying and preparing to go into the office one morning when the phone rang. It was Buddy, and I could hear the concern in his voice when he said, "We've got a problem. Checks are bouncing and creditors are calling."

Immediately, I started praying in tongues. I didn't want my mind to start thinking about all the "what ifs," "whys," and "what are we going to do?" stuff. The spirit man needed to be in control so that we could hear God's voice and walk victoriously through the problem.

All the way to work, I prayed in tongues. When I got there, we went into Buddy's office and prayed some more. Isaiah 26:3 (NKJV) says, *"You will keep him in perfect peace, whose mind is stayed on You, because he trusts in You."* We needed to pray so that we could get our minds on God and keep them there to stay in peace.

As we prayed, it was as if a blanket of peace were laid around us. We weren't worried or fearful. We knew that God would work out the situation and that the company would not be harmed.

It turned out that the bookkeeper had embezzled some funds. When we confronted the person in love, we discovered that the money had been stolen so this person could give to other ministries. This person's spouse wasn't saved and would not permit any tithes or offerings to be given. In order to get money to give, this person embezzled funds from the company.

As Buddy and I continued to pray and keep our minds on God and trust Him for a solution, He led us not to prosecute this person. The witness of the peaceful and loving way in which we handled the problem caused this person's unbelieving spouse to get saved. God blessed us and turned things around for the company because we chose to walk in faith, love, and peace by the power of the Holy Spirit.

Regardless of how difficult your situation is, you can have peace.

Jesus said, "I'm leaving you *My* peace." Jesus doesn't lie. He keeps His Word. If He said He left us peace, then He did. He told the disciples exactly what they had to do to remain in peace. They had to stop allowing themselves to be agitated, disturbed, fearful, intimidated, cowardly, and unsettled. They were responsible for maintaining peace—Jesus expected them to do it.

> *You will be secure under a government that is just and fair. Your enemies will stay far away. You will live in peace, and terror will not come near* (Isaiah 54:14 NLT).

You and I are responsible to maintain Jesus' peace in our lives. How do you keep from losing your peace? By knowing the Word of God and fellowshipping with Him through prayer, praise, and worship. No situation is ever as bad as your mind wants you to believe it is. When the devil gets hold of your mind, he sends outrageous thoughts. The more we allow our carnal minds to rule us, the more unrest we will experience.

Jesus said we need to stop allowing these things to attack us. What do we do when all kinds of thoughts flood our minds and fear tries to take control of us? We must get into the Word of God and speak to our minds and the fear that is trying to control us. We need to tell our minds to be quiet and listen to the Word of God.

Once we get our minds under control, we will become aware of His peace working in us. Jesus said the Holy Spirit would bring all things to our remembrance. If we have not put the Word of God inside us, we won't have anything for the Holy Spirit to bring to our remembrance. So we must meditate on and memorize the Word of God.

When we find ourselves in the midst of unpeace and unrest, we must speak the Word of God, letting it come out of our mouths. Hearing the Word is important because what we hear determines how we will act. The more we speak God's Word, the more we will walk in these truths on a daily basis. Then no matter what happens, we will maintain our love, joy, and peace, because we have spent time in His presence, studying and meditating on His Word.

Peace is already on the inside of us because Jesus is on the inside of us. Therefore, getting into His Word and His presence makes us aware once again of that peace. Peace will envelop us from the top of our heads to the soles of our feet. As we focus on Jesus and His Word, we will get our peace back. Then we can hear the Spirit of God and receive the answers we need.

It is part of our destiny to bring the hurting world that is lost and dying into the kingdom of God, where there is rest, peace, joy, righteousness, and deliverance. He gives us His Word and His truth so that we can take the steps necessary to walk out our deliverance and fulfill our destiny.

Trust in the Lord with all your heart, and lean not on your own understanding; in all your ways acknowledge Him, and He shall direct your paths. Do not be wise in your own eyes; fear the Lord and depart from evil. It will be health to your flesh, and strength to your bones (Proverbs 3:5-8 NKJV).

Chapter 9

KNOWLEDGE OF GOD PRODUCES PEACE

There is an old saying, "Ignorance is bliss." But that is a lie. Ignorance doesn't produce bliss or peace. It produces more problems.

We think that ignoring a situation will keep the peace, but it doesn't. God doesn't want us to ignore reality. He wants us to face reality from

139

His perspective and authority. That is what will produce peace.

Ignorance means a lack of knowledge. It's not that a person can't learn. He has just chosen not to learn. Hosea 4:6 (NLT) says, *"My people are being destroyed because they don't know me."*

God does not want us to walk in ignorance. He wants us to walk in the knowledge of who He is in His Word. Jesus and His Word are one.

This is the message of Good News for the people of Israel—that there is peace with God through Jesus Christ, who is Lord of all (Acts 10:36 NLT).

Therefore, we cannot remain peaceful due to our ignorance of what the Word says. Somewhere along the way, a circumstance or situation is going to catch up with us, and it's not going to be easy or fun if we don't have knowledge of God and His Word.

We need to understand that when God speaks peace out of His being, He creates peace. When He speaks, there's always spirit and life.

> *It is the Spirit Who gives life [He is the Life-giver]; the flesh conveys no benefit whatever [there is no profit in it]. The words (truths) that I have been speaking to you are spirit and life* (John 6:63 AMPC).

We need to ask ourselves if we are receiving or have ever received what Jesus said. We won't be able to maintain peace if we are not. If we are looking into the Word, we are looking at Jesus. If we are seeking Jesus, we are seeking the Word. Then there will be peace, because Jesus is— not has been, not will be, but *is* now this day and tomorrow—*peace*. He lives on the inside of us, so we have to awaken to the reality that true inner peace and true peace of mind is possible if we receive it through the Word of God and the Lord Jesus Christ because He is the Prince of Peace.

God doesn't just speak to communicate; He speaks to create. When He speaks peace, He creates peace, because He is a Creator. We need to speak the Word of God. We need to say what the Spirit of the Lord is saying to us about our lives and about us, so we can fully oper-ate in His peace. Not sometimes, not maybe, but *always*. When Jesus speaks or we speak His words, there's always spirit and life.

Everything that Jesus speaks or we hear by the Spirit of God is spirit and life because it comes from God, who is truth. Jesus is truth. There is no other truth higher than God, *none*. There is no other truth stronger than God, *none*. There is no other power stronger than God, *none*.

Much of the time, our minds dwell on our circumstances and what's happening to us. As a result, we begin to believe more in the devil and his power. Then we exalt our circumstance or situation by talking about it more than we do the power of God. The power of God is above any power that we can ever come in contact with. We need to get an understanding of this concept. There is no power stronger than the power of God, and there's no name more effective and stronger than the name of Jesus. Why? Because He is alive!

We need to look fully into the face of God and into the Word of God for understanding in order to receive the contentment and peace that He intends for us. There's a difference in being content and being in a comfort zone. There's a big difference. A lot of times, we stay in our comfort zone because it's comfortable. We don't have to *stretch* ourselves in any way. We don't have to stretch our physical abilities.

We don't have to stretch our spiritual abilities. We don't have to stretch our mental abilities. We can just float along in our comfort zone.

It's possible to be in a comfort zone and still not be content because contentment comes from peace. We have to truly want to make a difference in our lives through our circumstances. We have to see Jesus. In order to help someone else, they have to see Jesus in us.

How are they going to see Jesus in us? They will see Jesus in us through our lives—His life in us. They are going to see Jesus in us through the love, joy, and peace that we reflect in our lives. When we operate in the freedom that Jesus has given us and turn our minds toward Him and His Word, we will receive the peace we need from Him in our minds.

It's not hard to receive and maintain peace for our spirit, but it is for our minds. That's why we must allow the spirit man to rule. We control our minds by renewing them with the

Word of God daily. We can't wait until we face a crisis to begin renewing our minds—it will be too late. We need to have knowledge of God's Word before the temptations and trials come.

A lot of times we just try to worry our way out of situations. We think, *Well, if we do this… or what about that…I don't know.* Our minds just keep going over the situation, and the more the mind goes over it, the bigger the problem becomes. That's what worry does. It magnifies the situation, makes the problem bigger than God.

Worry is the opposite of meditation. When we worry, we are trying to solve the problem all by ourselves. Since we are relying on ourselves, we worry about the situation and contemplate it until it becomes a stronghold in us and we become discouraged or defeated. If we worry, we are not allowing the power of the Spirit and the Word to operate in us to stop the confusion and irritation.

On the other hand, when we meditate on the Word, knowledge comes and we are encouraged. We are uplifted and can see Jesus through the circumstance or situation. We are responsible for our world so we have to confer with Jesus to stop confusion and agitation. We need to stop allowing ourselves to be troubled. We have to do it. We need to meditate and confess the words of Jesus. He told the disciples:

> *Peace I leave with you; My [own] peace I now give and bequeath to you. Not as the world gives do I give to you. Do not let your hearts be troubled, neither let them be afraid. [Stop allowing yourselves to be agitated and disturbed; and do not permit yourselves to be fearful and intimidated and cowardly and unsettled]* (John 14:27 AMPC).

He also told the disciples:

I have told you these things, so that in Me you may have [perfect] peace and confidence. In the world you have tribulation and trials and distress and frustration; but be of good cheer [take courage; be confident, certain, undaunted]! For I have overcome the world. [I have deprived it of power to harm you and have conquered it for you] (John 16:33 AMPC).

You need to tell yourself, *I will* not *be agitated, disturbed, fearful, intimidated, cowardly, or unsettled, because I live and move and have my being in Jesus. Jesus is the Prince of Peace. He is my victory. Therefore, I have peace and victory.*

Jesus said, "I have deprived it of power to harm you and have conquered it for you." The devil may come in all sorts of ways to try to discourage and defeat us, but we need to realize what Jesus has done for us. The Word of God says that Jesus Christ has come and given us peace. It also says that He has deprived the world of power to harass us and has already conquered it for us.

> *And do not be conformed to this world, but be transformed by the renewing of your mind, that you may prove what is that good and acceptable and perfect will of God* (Romans 12:2 NKJV).

The reason we dwell on the negative when something happens is because we allow fear to take hold of us instead of staying in rest, peace, and quietness. For example, when we have children who don't quite understand the situation, we spend all of our time comforting them and don't have time to comfort ourselves. But if we use the Word of God to comfort our children, it will comfort us also.

We have to begin to see where we need to look. Do we need to look at the world or do we need to look in the Bible? When we continually look to Jesus and His Word, we are more than conquerors. Peace comes when we speak and quote the Word. When we cultivate the Word of God that has been placed within us, we keep our hearts and minds from being troubled.

When something is cultivated, it is plowed up, smoothed out, and plowed up again, getting rid of the rocks and anything that would hinder or deter growth.

It's important for us to cultivate the Word in us. We need to have that continual cultivation of the Word to pull up and root out all those things in us that deter us from completely accomplishing what God said we could. The Word of God is not new; it's been around a long time. It is made fresh by the Spirit of God. For example, I can listen to a message in the morning and get so much out of it. Then I can hear it again in the evening and get even more out of it.

When we allow the Word of God to live and abide in us and we abide in Him, we will walk in peace. Sometimes we wonder why more Christians are not experiencing peace on a daily basis. Many times, they don't want to get close enough to God to hear what He is saying to them, because they are concerned that it may not be what they want to hear.

Many people anchor their peace in their job, 401K, or investment portfolio. All of these things are important, but focusing on them will not sustain peace. "*Which hope we have as an anchor of the soul, both sure and stedfast, and which entereth into that within the veil*" (Hebrews 6:19 KJV). The New Living Translation says, "*This hope is a strong and trustworthy anchor for our souls. It leads us through the curtain into God's inner sanctuary.*" Beck's says, "which (hope) we have an anchor of the soul…like an anchor for our lives."

When we build a relationship with Him through the Word of God and prayer, He is going to speak to us and direct our lives. We will know the will of God for our lives. We might not know every aspect of it immediately, but as we seek Him on a daily basis He will lead us step by step. He has a purpose and plan for our lives. But we cannot get in a hurry. Remember, it's not our plan; it's His.

Finally, brethren, whatsoever things are true, whatsoever things are honest, whatsoever things are just, whatsoever things are pure, whatsoever things are lovely, whatsoever things are of good report; if there be any virtue, and if there be any praise, think on these things (Philippians 4:8 KJV).

We have to renew our minds with the Word of God on a daily basis. The Word of God is the avenue we use in order to get to know Him. We have to renew our minds with the Word. Our hearts have peace when we come into the kingdom of God because Jesus is there and He is peace. He is the Prince of Peace.

Our spirits have peace but our minds don't always stay *on* that peace or *in* that peace. Renewing our minds is so important because it's our minds that give us trouble. Many times when our minds hear the Word of God, that Word is contrary to what the mind is used to hearing or doing and therefore it wants to rebel. When we listen to our minds, our bodies will side right in with that wrong thinking and we will become rebellious. The world's way of thinking is contrary to the Word of God.

I'm so glad that He is the Prince of Peace and He lives on the inside of us. We can walk in that peace every day, but we must choose to do so. We must continually renew our minds to the Word of God in order to get rid of those ugly thought patterns that lead us into unrest and unpeace. Then we will be victorious and more than conquerors through Christ Jesus.

This wonderful peace of God will allow us to stay in rest. He is our peace and tranquility of heart and mind. We can maintain that peace in our hearts easily because the spirit man has been redeemed and made whole. It is brand-new. But we also have to maintain that peace in our minds in order to maintain it in our bodies. We have to know the Word of God and speak it. This will bring peace and help us keep it.

If we allow our minds to rule us, we will live in fear and unrest. Since we have the Word of God and the Holy Spirit, we know that it doesn't matter how things look in the world, because we walk in the victory of the Lord Jesus Christ. He overcame, so we are overcomers. He conquered all, so we are more than conquerors through Him. Jesus is our peace; therefore, we have peace.

ABOUT PAT HARRISON

If one phrase could describe the life and ministry of Pat Harrison, it would be, "I love the Holy Ghost." Anytime she makes that statement, Pat goes on to say, "I love the Holy Ghost because He is everything to me Jesus said He would be."

Throughout her life and walk with God, Pat has learned that God is faithful and that the Word of God is true. Together, she and her husband, Buddy, have pioneered churches, built successful businesses, and led Faith Christian Fellowship International.

Pat was reminded of the faithfulness of God when Buddy went home to be with the Lord in November 1998. She continues to lead the ministry, and travel sharing the truth of God's Word.

Pat is a successful author, speaker, and leader. Her insights into the Word of God and her lifelong personal walk with the Holy Spirit are an inspiration to those she ministers to and touches with her life.

Pat has written several books that have been distributed throughout the world. Her writings and speaking ministry encourage people to develop a personal walk with God and get to know the person of the Holy Spirit.